Italian

easy, fresh & flavoursome

THE AUSTRALIAN
Women's Weekly

CONTENTS

antipasto	4
antipasto favourites	10
starters	12
salads	18
salad favourites	20
pizzas	22
pasta & risotto	26
pasta favourites	36
mains	38
desserts	66
dessert favourites	72
glossary	74
conversion chart	77
index	78

AUSTRALIAN CUP AND
SPOON MEASUREMENTS
ARE METRIC.
A CONVERSION CHART
APPEARS ON PAGE 77.

When we think of Italian food, heavy lasagnes and creamy pasta dishes often spring to mind. Although comforting and delicious, these hearty, rich meals are only a part of what Italian cuisine has to offer. This little book is full of light, elegant Italian recipes with gorgeous fresh flavour combinations. You'll be inspired.

Pamela Clark

Food Director

ARANCINI

prep + cook time 1 hour 30 minutes (+ cooling) **makes** 24
nutritional count per arancini 5.7g total fat
(1.8g saturated fat); 401kJ (96 cal);
8.1g carbohydrate; 1.9g protein; 1g fibre

2 cups (500ml) chicken stock
½ cup (125ml) dry white wine
45g (1½ ounces) butter
1 small brown onion (80g), chopped finely
1 clove garlic, crushed
1 cup (200g) arborio rice
⅓ cup (25g) finely grated parmesan cheese
⅓ cup (35g) coarsely grated
    mozzarella cheese
24 fetta-stuffed green olives (240g)
⅓ cup (35g) packaged breadcrumbs
vegetable oil, for deep-frying

1 Combine stock and wine in medium
saucepan; bring to the boil. Reduce heat;
simmer, covered.
2 Meanwhile, melt butter in medium saucepan;
cook onion and garlic, stirring, until onion
softens. Add rice; stir over medium heat until
rice is coated in butter mixture. Stir in ½ cup of
the simmering stock mixture; cook, stirring,
over low heat until liquid is absorbed. Continue
adding stock mixture, in ½-cup batches,
stirring, until absorbed after each addition.
Total cooking time should be about 35 minutes
or until rice is tender. Stir in cheeses; season to
taste. Cover; cool 30 minutes.
3 Roll rounded tablespoons of risotto
mixture into balls; press an olive into centre
of each ball, roll to enclose. Coat risotto balls
in breadcrumbs.
4 Heat oil in wok; deep-fry risotto balls, in
batches, until browned lightly. Drain on
absorbent paper.

ANTIPASTO

artichokes with lemon caper dressing

MARINATED MUSHROOMS

prep + cook time **40 minutes** makes **4 cups**
nutritional count per ¼ cup 28.6g total fat
(4g saturated fat); 1145kJ (274 cal);
0.2g carbohydrate; 1.9g protein; 1.3g fibre

1 litre (4 cups) white vinegar
1 cup (250ml) dry white wine
1 tablespoon sea salt flakes
750g (1½ pounds) button mushrooms, halved
2 cloves garlic, sliced thinly
½ teaspoon dried chilli flakes
1 tablespoon coarsely chopped
    fresh rosemary
1 tablespoon finely chopped fresh
    flat-leaf parsley
3 x 5cm (2-inch) strips lemon rind
1 dried bay leaf
2 cups (500ml) olive oil

1 Sterilise 1-litre (4-cup) jar and lid.
2 Heat vinegar, wine and half the salt in
medium saucepan without boiling. Add
mushrooms; simmer, uncovered, about
5 minutes or until tender. Drain mushrooms;
discard liquid.
3 Place hot mushrooms in large heatproof
bowl with garlic, chilli, herbs, rind, bay leaf
and remaining salt; toss to combine. Spoon
mushroom mixture into hot sterilised jar.
4 Heat oil in small saucepan; carefully pour into
jar to completely cover mushrooms, leaving a
1cm (½-inch) space between mushrooms and
top of jar. Seal while hot.

tips To sterilise jar and lid, place in the dishwasher on
the hottest rinse cycle. Don't use detergent.
Alternatively, lay the jar and lid in a large pan, cover
completely with cold water and bring gradually to the
boil; boil for 20 minutes. Store marinated mushrooms in
refrigerator for up to three months. Serve mushrooms
with crusty bread or as part of an antipasto platter with
cheeses and deli meats.

ARTICHOKES
WITH LEMON CAPER DRESSING

prep + cook time **1 hour** serves **4**
nutritional count per serving 28.8g total fat
(4g saturated fat); 1304kJ (312 cal);
3.4g carbohydrate; 4.1g protein; 11.3g fibre

4 medium globe artichokes (800g)
½ cup (125ml) lemon juice
½ cup (125ml) light olive oil
2 cloves garlic, crushed
2 tablespoons drained capers, rinsed,
    chopped coarsely
¼ cup coarsely chopped fresh
    flat-leaf parsley

1 Trim artichoke stalks to 1cm (½ inch);
remove tough outer leaves. Cut 2.5cm (1 inch)
off the top of artichokes. Using small spoon,
scoop out furry chokes in centre of artichokes.
2 Place artichokes, cut-side down, in steamer.
Steam artichokes, covered tightly, about
45 minutes or until stems are tender; cut
artichokes in half. Place hot artichokes on
serving plates; drizzle with combined remaining
ingredients. Season to taste.

marinated mushrooms

GIARDINIERA (PICKLED VEGETABLES)

prep + cook time **1 hour** makes **6 cups**
nutritional count per ¼ cup **19.1g total fat**
(2.7g saturated fat); 748kJ (179 cal);
1.6g carbohydrate; 0.7g protein; 1g fibre

2 medium red capsicums (bell peppers) (400g)
1 litre (4 cups) white vinegar
2 cups (500ml) water
6 black peppercorns
1 dried bay leaf
1 tablespoon sea salt flakes
1 small eggplant (230g), quartered
   lengthways, cut into 1cm (½-inch) slices
½ small cauliflower (200g), cut into florets
2 medium carrots (240g), sliced thinly on
   the diagonal
2 stalks celery (300g), sliced thickly on
   the diagonal
2 tablespoons finely chopped fresh
   flat-leaf parsley
2 teaspoons finely chopped fresh thyme
2 cups (500ml) olive oil
2 cloves garlic, sliced thinly

1 Preheat oven to 200°C/400°F. Sterilise
1.5-litre (6-cup) jar and lid.
2 Quarter capsicums; discard seeds and
membranes. Roast capsicum, skin-side up,
until skin blisters and blackens. Cover
capsicum with plastic wrap or paper for 5
minutes; peel away skin then slice thickly.
3 Meanwhile, combine vinegar, the water,
peppercorns, bay leaf and half the salt in large
saucepan; heat without boiling. Add eggplant,
cauliflower, carrot and celery; bring to the boil.
Reduce heat; simmer, uncovered, about 5
minutes or until vegetables are tender. Drain
vegetables; discard liquid.
4 Combine hot vegetables, capsicum, herbs
and remaining salt in large heatproof bowl.
Spoon vegetable mixture into sterilised jar.
5 Heat oil and garlic in small saucepan, strain
into large heatproof jug; discard garlic. Carefully
pour hot oil over vegetables in jar to completely
cover vegetables, leaving a 1cm (½-inch) space
between vegetables and top of jar. Seal while hot.

tip To sterilise jar and lid, place in the dishwasher on
the hottest rinse cycle. Don't use detergent.
Alternatively, lay the jar and lid in a large pan, cover
completely with cold water and bring gradually to the
boil; boil for 20 minutes. Store giardiniera in the
refrigerator for up to three months.

CHERRY TOMATO & PARMESAN DIP

prep + cook time **35 minutes** serves **6**
nutritional count per serving **12.6g total fat**
(6.9g saturated fat); 932kJ (223 cal);
20g carbohydrate; 6.4g protein; 2.4g fibre

Preheat oven to 220°C/425°F. Combine 250g
(8 ounces) cherry tomatoes and 2 teaspoons
olive oil on oven tray; roast, uncovered, about
15 minutes or until tomato skins split. Cool
10 minutes. Combine tomatoes, ½ cup sour
cream, ½ cup finely grated parmesan cheese,
2 tablespoons finely chopped fresh basil and
½ teaspoon dried chilli flakes in medium bowl;
season to taste. Thinly slice 1 stick sourdough
bread; toast bread both sides. Rub toasts with
2 halved garlic cloves; serve with tomato and
parmesan dip.

CHUNKY OLIVE AND HERB DIP

prep time **20 minutes** makes **1½ cups**
nutritional count per teaspoon **1.6g total fat**
(0.2g saturated fat); 67kJ (16 cal);
0.3g carbohydrate; 0.1g protein; 0.1g fibre

Combine ½ cup finely chopped seeded green
olives, ½ cup each finely chopped fresh flat-leaf
parsley and mint, ¼ cup finely chopped fresh
dill, 6 finely chopped drained anchovy fillets,
2 teaspoons finely grated lemon rind, ¼ cup
lemon juice and ½ cup olive oil in medium
bowl; season to taste.

ANTIPASTO FAVOURITES

WARM OLIVES WITH CHILLI

prep + cook time **10 minutes** serves **8**
nutritional count per serving **21.2g total fat**
(3g saturated fat); 1037kJ (248 cal);
14.1g carbohydrate; 0.5g protein; 0.8g fibre

Gently heat ¾ cup extra virgin olive oil in large
frying pan, add 1 thinly sliced fresh long red
chilli, 1 thinly sliced garlic clove and ¼ cup
coarsely chopped fresh oregano; stir until warm
and fragrant. Add 500g (1 pound) black and
green olives; shake the pan until heated
through. Season to taste. Serve olives with
grissini, if you like.

MELON IN PROSCIUTTO

prep time **15 minutes** serves **4**
nutritional count per serving **11.9g total fat**
(2.2g saturated fat); 623kJ (149 cal);
10.9g carbohydrate; 9.4g protein; 2.5g fibre

Halve 1 small rockmelon lengthways. Peel and
seed then cut into 12 wedges. Wrap 12 slices
prosciutto around melon wedges; drizzle with
2 tablespoons olive oil, sprinkle with ¼ cup
loosely packed fresh flat-leaf parsley leaves.

tip **Use a good quality extra virgin olive oil for the
best flavour.**

SICILIAN ZUCCHINI FLOWERS

prep + cook time 30 minutes serves 12
nutritional count per serving 6.9g total fat
(2.3g saturated fat); 351kJ (84 cal);
4.1g carbohydrate; 1.2g protein; 1g fibre

2 tablespoons olive oil
40g (1½ ounces) butter
2 slices ciabatta bread (70g), crusts
   removed, chopped finely
2 cloves garlic, crushed
1 tablespoon roasted pine nuts,
   chopped coarsely
1 tablespoon finely grated lemon rind
2 tablespoons finely chopped fresh
   flat-leaf parsley
1 tablespoon dried currants
24 baby zucchini with flowers
   attached (400g)

1 Heat half the oil and half the butter in large
frying pan. Add bread; cook, stirring, until
browned lightly. Add garlic; cook, stirring, until
fragrant. Stir in nuts, rind, parsley and currants.
Remove from pan.
2 Heat remaining oil and butter in pan.
Add zucchini; cook, turning gently, until just
tender. Serve zucchini sprinkled with crisped
bread mixture.

tip If baby zucchini with the flowers attached are
not available, replace with small zucchini cut into
quartered lengths.

STARTERS

beef carpaccio

BRUSCHETTA WITH TOMATO, BASIL AND CAPERS

prep + cook time **15 minutes** serves **6**
nutritional count per serving **8.5g total fat**
(1.2g saturated fat); 1241kJ (297 cal);
42.5g carbohydrate; 9.5g protein; 5.5g fibre

1.5kg (3 pounds) ripe tomatoes
2 tablespoons extra virgin olive oil
¼ cup loosely packed fresh baby
**   basil leaves**
2 tablespoons drained baby capers, rinsed
500g (1 pound) loaf wood-fired bread
1 clove garlic, halved

1 Seed and finely chop tomatoes; combine in
medium bowl with oil, basil and capers.
Season to taste.
2 Cut bread into 12 slices; toast slices both
sides on heated oiled grill plate (or grill or
barbecue). Rub one side of each slice with the
cut side of a garlic clove; place toast on platter,
garlic-side up.
3 Top toasts with tomato mixture; sprinkle with
freshly ground black pepper and drizzle with a
little extra olive oil.

BEEF CARPACCIO

prep time **30 minutes (+ freezing)** serves **8**
nutritional count per serving **7.8g total fat**
(2.3g saturated fat); 506kJ (121 cal);
0.3g carbohydrate; 12.3g protein; 0.3g fibre

400g (12½-ounce) piece beef eye fillet
2 tablespoons olive oil
2 teaspoons finely grated lemon rind
2 tablespoons lemon juice
1 clove garlic, crushed
⅓ cup finely chopped fresh flat-leaf parsley
2 tablespoons finely chopped fresh oregano
⅓ cup finely chopped baby rocket
**   (arugula) leaves**
⅓ cup (25g) flaked parmesan cheese

1 Tightly wrap beef fillet in plastic wrap; freeze
1 hour or until firm.
2 Unwrap beef; slice as thinly as possible.
Arrange slices on platter.
3 Combine olive oil, rind, juice, garlic, herbs
and rocket in small bowl; season to taste.
4 Serve beef sprinkled with herb mixture
and cheese.

bruschetta with tomato, basil and capers

SARDINE SKEWERS WITH GREMOLATA DRESSING

prep + cook time **35 minutes** makes **10**
nutritional count per skewer **9g total fat**
(1.6g saturated fat); 464kJ (111 cal);
0.3g carbohydrate; 6.9g protein; 0.7g fibre

1 cup firmly packed fresh flat-leaf parsley
  leaves, chopped coarsely
⅓ cup coarsely chopped preserved
  lemon rind
¼ cup (60ml) mustard seed oil
4 cloves garlic, crushed
10 butterflied sardines (300g)

1 Make gremolata dressing by combining
parsley, preserved lemon rind, oil and garlic in
small bowl.
2 Meanwhile, thread sardines onto metal
skewers; cook on heated oiled barbecue (or
grill or grill pan). Season; serve with dressing.

tip You can buy butterflied sardines from most good
fish markets, or get your fishmonger to butterfly the fish
for you. To butterfly your own fish, buy an already gutted
fish, slice down the length of the belly until just before
the tail, place fish, belly-down, on a chopping board and
roll gently with a rolling pin several times to flatten, pull
head gently up and away towards the tail, removing
head and bones together.

BEAN SALAD WITH MOZZARELLA, SUN-DRIED TOMATO AND OLIVES

prep + cook time 20 minutes **serves** 4
nutritional count per serving 16.6g total fat
(5.1g saturated fat); 1438kJ (344 cal);
28g carbohydrate; 15.6g protein; 10.5g fibre

200g (6½ ounces) green beans,
  halved crossways
800g (1½ pounds) canned four-bean mix,
  rinsed, drained
2 teaspoons each finely chopped fresh
  thyme and oregano
⅓ cup coarsely chopped fresh
  flat-leaf parsley
100g (3 ounces) mozzarella cheese,
  sliced thickly
¾ cup (110g) drained sun-dried tomatoes,
  sliced thinly
1 medium brown onion (150g), sliced thinly
1 cup (120g) seeded black olives
italian dressing
1 clove garlic, crushed
2 tablespoons olive oil
2 tablespoons lemon juice

1 Combine ingredients for italian dressing in
screw-top jar; shake well.
2 Boil, steam or microwave green beans until
tender; drain. Rinse under cold water; drain.
3 Combine green beans and four-bean mix in
medium bowl with remaining ingredients and
dressing; toss gently. Season to taste.

SALADS

CAPRESE SALAD WITH FIGS

prep time **20 minutes** serves **4**
nutritional count per serving **23.7g total fat**
(10.7g saturated fat); 1367kJ (327 cal);
8.8g carbohydrate; 18.5g protein; 3.4g fibre

Thinly slice 4 large tomatoes, 4 large fresh
figs and 375g (12 ounces) drained cherry
bocconcini cheeses. Finely chop ½ small
red onion. Overlap slices of tomato, fig and
cheese on serving plate. Sprinkle with onion
and ¼ cup firmly packed fresh basil leaves;
drizzle with combined 2 tablespoons olive oil
and 1 tablespoon balsamic vinegar. Season
to taste.

MUSHROOM & PANCETTA SALAD

prep + cook time **20 minutes** serves **6**
nutritional count per serving **6g total fat**
(1.5g saturated fat); 360kJ (86 cal);
1.3g carbohydrate; 5.6g protein; 1.6g fibre

Combine 200g (6½ ounces) quartered swiss
brown mushrooms with 2 tablespoons
balsamic vinegar in small bowl. Cook 8 slices
pancetta in medium oiled frying pan until
crisp; chop coarsely. Drain mushrooms;
discard vinegar. Cook mushrooms in same
pan until tender. Combine pancetta and
mushrooms with 1 tablespoon balsamic
vinegar, 100g (3 ounces) baby spinach leaves,
2 tablespoons rinsed and drained baby capers,
2 finely chopped green onions (scallions),
1 tablespoon olive oil and 1 crushed garlic
clove in large bowl; season to taste.

FIG & PROSCIUTTO SALAD

prep + cook time **15 minutes** serves **4**
nutritional count per serving **16.9g total fat**
(5.7g saturated fat); 1062kJ (254 cal);
13.7g carbohydrate; 11.1g protein; 2.6g fibre

Preheat grill (broiler). Grill 6 slices prosciutto
until crisp; chop coarsely. Combine ¼ cup
cider vinegar, 2 tablespoons olive oil,
1 tablespoon wholegrain mustard and
1 tablespoon honey in screw-top jar; shake
well, season to taste. Serve 120g (4 ounces)
baby rocket (arugula) leaves topped with
4 quartered large fresh figs, 150g (4½ ounces)
crumbled soft goat's cheese and prosciutto;
drizzle with dressing.

tip **Freeze cheese for 10 minutes to make**
crumbling easier.

ROCKET & PARMESAN SALAD

prep time **10 minutes** serves **4**
nutritional count per serving **12.3g total fat**
(2.3g saturated fat); 635kJ (152 cal);
4.4g carbohydrate; 5.1g protein; 2.2g fibre

Combine 1 tablespoon balsamic vinegar,
1 tablespoon olive oil, 100g (3 ounces) baby
rocket (arugula) leaves, 2 tablespoons roasted
pine nuts, ¼ cup coarsely chopped drained
semi-dried tomatoes and ⅓ cup flaked
parmesan cheese in large bowl; toss gently.
Season to taste.

FIG, PROSCIUTTO AND GOAT'S CHEESE PIZZETTAS

prep + cook time 1 hour (+ standing) serves 4
nutritional count per serving 11g total fat
(4.3g saturated fat); 1898kJ (454 cal);
66.4g carbohydrate; 19.2g protein; 5.8g fibre

⅓ cup (85g) bottled tomato pasta sauce
125g (4 ounces) soft goat's cheese, crumbled
2 large fresh figs (160g), cut into thin wedges
4 slices prosciutto (60g), chopped coarsely
30g (1 ounce) baby rocket (arugula) leaves
pizza dough
2 teaspoons (7g) instant yeast
½ teaspoon salt
2½ cups (375g) plain (all-purpose) flour
1 cup (250ml) warm water
1 tablespoon olive oil

1 Make pizza dough.
2 Preheat barbecue or grill plate to medium heat.
3 Divide dough into four portions; roll each portion into 15cm (6-inch) round pizzetta base. Cover barbecue grill plate with double thickness of oiled foil. Place pizzetta bases on foil; cook 5 minutes.
4 Using metal tongs, turn bases; spread cooked side with pasta sauce, season. Divide cheese, fig and prosciutto between bases. Cook, covered, over low heat about 5 minutes or until bases are cooked through. Just before serving, top with rocket.
pizza dough Combine yeast, salt and sifted flour in large bowl; gradually stir in combined water and oil. Knead dough on floured surface about 10 minutes or until smooth and elastic. Place dough in large oiled bowl; cover, stand in warm place about 30 minutes or until dough doubles in size. Punch down dough with fist; knead dough on floured surface until smooth.

tip Use bought small (15cm/6-inch) pizza bases if you like.

PIZZAS

potato and rosemary pizza

POTATO AND ROSEMARY PIZZA

prep + cook time **45 minutes (+ standing)** serves **6**
nutritional count per serving **7g total fat**
(1g saturated fat); 1367kJ (327 cal);
54.5g carbohydrate; 8.9g protein; 4.1g fibre

2 tablespoons olive oil
410g (13 ounces) baby new potatoes,
 sliced thinly
1 clove garlic, crushed
1 tablespoon coarsely chopped
 fresh rosemary
pizza dough
1 cup (250ml) warm water
1 teaspoon caster (superfine) sugar
2 teaspoons (7g) instant yeast
2½ cups (375g) plain (all-purpose) flour
1 teaspoon coarse cooking salt (kosher salt)

1 Make pizza dough.
2 Preheat oven to 220°C/425°F. Oil two
oven trays.
3 Divide dough in half. Roll each portion into
18cm x 30cm (7-inch x 12-inch) rectangles;
place on trays. Brush pizza bases with half
the oil.
4 Combine potatoes, garlic, rosemary and
remaining oil in medium bowl, season; layer
potato mixture evenly over bases.
5 Bake pizzas about 30 minutes or
until browned.

pizza dough Combine the water, sugar and
yeast in small jug. Stand in warm place about
10 minutes or until frothy. Sift flour and salt
into large bowl, add yeast mixture; mix to a
soft dough. Knead dough on floured surface
about 10 minutes or until smooth and elastic.
Place dough in oiled large bowl. Cover; stand
in warm place about 1 hour or until doubled
in size.

fennel and ricotta pizza

FENNEL AND RICOTTA PIZZA

prep + cook time **40 minutes** serves **4**
nutritional count per serving **17.4g total fat**
(10g saturated fat); 1827kJ (437 cal);
51.8g carbohydrate; 15.6g protein; 5.9g fibre

45g (1½ ounces) butter
2 medium fennel bulbs (600g), sliced thinly
½ teaspoon brown mustard seeds
1 teaspoon finely grated lemon rind
1 tablespoon lemon juice
1 teaspoon thinly sliced orange rind
1 tablespoon orange juice
4 large pitta breads (320g)
1 cup (260g) bottled tomato pasta sauce
1 cup (240g) ricotta cheese
1 tablespoon fennel fronds

1 Preheat oven to 220°C/425°F.
2 Heat butter in large frying pan; cook fennel,
stirring occasionally, until tender. Stir in seeds,
rinds and juices. Season to taste.
3 Place pitta on oven trays; spread with pasta
sauce. Divide fennel mixture between pitta;
sprinkle with cheese.
4 Bake pizzas about 10 minutes or until pitta
bases are crisp and topping is heated through.
Just before serving, sprinkle with fennel fronds.

BAKED ASPARAGUS RISOTTO

prep + cook time 1 hour 10 minutes serves 4
nutritional count per serving 8g total fat
(2.5g saturated fat); 1262kJ (388 cal);
65.2g carbohydrate; 11.5g protein; 2.7g fibre

3½ cups (875ml) chicken or vegetable stock
2 teaspoons finely grated lemon rind
¼ cup (60ml) lemon juice
1 tablespoon olive oil
1 medium brown onion (150g),
   chopped finely
1 clove garlic, crushed
1½ cups (300g) arborio rice
170g (5½ ounces) asparagus,
   chopped coarsely
250g (8 ounces) cherry tomatoes, halved
⅓ cup (25g) finely grated parmesan cheese
2 teaspoons finely chopped fresh thyme

1 Preheat oven to 180°C/350°F.
2 Bring stock, rind and juice to the boil
in medium saucepan. Reduce heat;
simmer, covered.
3 Meanwhile, heat oil in medium saucepan;
cook onion and garlic, stirring, until onion
softens. Add rice; stir rice to coat in onion
mixture. Stir in simmering stock mixture.
4 Place risotto mixture in shallow large
ovenproof dish; cover with foil. Bake about
25 minutes, stirring halfway through cooking.
Add asparagus and tomato; bake, uncovered,
about 25 minutes or until rice is tender.
5 Remove from oven; season to taste. Serve
sprinkled with cheese and thyme.

tips Baked risotto is a delicious alternative to the usual
hand-stirred risotto (and a lot easier, too). Be sure to
cover the risotto mixture tightly with foil, while baking,
to ensure a perfectly creamy result.

PASTA &
RISOTTO

ricotta gnocchi with tomato sauce

RICOTTA GNOCCHI WITH TOMATO SAUCE

prep + cook time **1 hour** serves **4**
nutritional count per serving 34.3g total fat
(16.4g saturated fat); 2412kJ (577 cal);
30.6g carbohydrate; 29.8g protein; 3.9g fibre

2 tablespoons olive oil
1 small red onion (100g), chopped finely
1 clove garlic, crushed
800g (1½ pounds) canned diced tomatoes
2 teaspoons caster (superfine) sugar
½ cup (125ml) dry red wine
1 cup (240g) ricotta cheese
3 cups (240g) finely grated pecorino cheese
1 egg
pinch nutmeg
¾ cup (110g) plain (all-purpose) flour

1 Heat oil in large frying pan; cook onion
and garlic, stirring, until onion softens. Add
undrained tomato, sugar and wine; bring
to the boil. Reduce heat; simmer, uncovered,
about 30 minutes or until sauce thickens
slightly. Season to taste.
2 Meanwhile, stir ricotta, 2 cups of the
pecorino, egg, nutmeg and flour in large bowl
until mixture forms a soft dough. Divide
mixture into four portions; roll each portion on
a lightly floured surface into a 30cm (12-inch)
long sausage shape. Cut each sausage into
2.5cm (1-inch) gnocchi pieces; roll pieces
into balls. Flatten each ball slightly with the
palm of your hand.
3 Cook gnocchi, in two batches, in large
saucepan of boiling water about 3 minutes
or until gnocchi float to the surface.
Remove gnocchi from saucepan; drain on
absorbent paper.
4 Divide gnocchi between serving plates;
top with tomato sauce, sprinkle with
remaining pecorino.

SPAGHETTI NAPOLETANA

prep + cook time **30 minutes** serves **4**
nutritional count per serving 3.8g total fat
(0.5g saturated fat); 1630kJ (390 cal);
71.9g carbohydrate; 12.8g protein; 6.6g fibre

2 teaspoons olive oil
1 small brown onion (80g), chopped finely
3 cloves garlic, crushed
800g (1½ pounds) canned crushed tomatoes
¼ cup coarsely chopped fresh basil
⅓ cup coarsely chopped fresh
    flat-leaf parsley
375g (12 ounces) spaghetti

1 Heat oil in large saucepan; cook onion and
garlic, stirring, until onion softens. Add
undrained tomatoes; bring to the boil. Reduce
heat; simmer, uncovered, about 20 minutes or
until reduced by about a third. Stir in basil and
parsley; season to taste.
2 Meanwhile, cook pasta in large saucepan of
boiling water until tender; drain.
3 Serve pasta topped with sauce.

spaghetti napoletana

angel hair pasta with smoked salmon and asparagus

ANGEL HAIR PASTA WITH SMOKED SALMON AND ASPARAGUS

prep + cook time **15 minutes** serves **4**
nutritional count per serving **16.6g total fat**
(2.5g saturated fat); 2128kJ (509 cal);
66g carbohydrate; 20.9g protein; 4.7g fibre

375g (12 ounces) angel hair pasta
¼ cup (60ml) olive oil
250g (8 ounces) asparagus, trimmed,
    chopped coarsely
150g (4½ ounces) smoked salmon,
    sliced thinly
2 tablespoons drained baby capers, rinsed
½ cup finely chopped fresh chives
75g (2½ ounces) baby rocket (arugula) leaves
1 lemon, cut into wedges

1 Cook pasta in large saucepan of boiling water until tender; drain. Return pasta to pan.
2 Meanwhile, heat oil in small frying pan; cook asparagus, stirring, until tender.
3 Add asparagus, salmon, capers, chives and rocket to pasta; season to taste, toss gently to combine. Serve pasta with lemon wedges.

PRAWN AND ASPARAGUS RISOTTO

prep + cook time **1 hour 10 minutes** serves **4**
nutritional count per serving **14.7g total fat**
(5.5g saturated fat); 2516kJ (602 cal);
82.8g carbohydrate; 26.3g protein; 2.6g fibre

500g (1 pound) uncooked medium king
    prawns (shrimp)
3 cups (750ml) chicken stock
3 cups (750ml) water
15g (½ ounce) butter
1 tablespoon olive oil
1 small brown onion (80g), chopped finely
2 cups (400g) arborio rice
½ cup (125ml) dry sherry
15g (½ ounce) butter, extra
2 teaspoons olive oil, extra
2 cloves garlic, crushed
500g (1 pound) asparagus, chopped coarsely
⅓ cup (25g) coarsely grated
    parmesan cheese
⅓ cup coarsely chopped fresh basil

prawn and asparagus risotto

1 Shell and devein prawns; chop prawn meat coarsely.
2 Place stock and the water in large saucepan; bring to the boil. Reduce heat; simmer, covered.
3 Meanwhile, heat butter and oil in large saucepan; cook onion, stirring, until softened. Add rice; stir rice to coat in onion mixture. Add sherry; cook, stirring, until liquid is almost evaporated.
4 Stir in 1 cup simmering stock mixture; cook, stirring, over low heat until liquid is absorbed. Continue adding stock mixture, in 1-cup batches, stirring, until absorbed after each addition. Total cooking time should be about 35 minutes or until rice is tender.
5 Heat extra butter and extra oil in medium frying pan; cook prawn meat and garlic, stirring, until prawn just changes colour.
6 Boil, steam or microwave asparagus until tender; drain. Add asparagus, prawn mixture and cheese to risotto; cook, stirring, until cheese melts. Stir in basil; season to taste.

SPINACH AND RICOTTA CANNELLONI

prep + cook time **1 hour** serves **6**
nutritional count per serving **31g total fat**
(17.1g saturated fat); 2412kJ (577 cal);
41.8g carbohydrate; 28.7g protein; 8.3g fibre

1kg (2 pounds) spinach, trimmed,
    chopped coarsely
500g (1 pound) ricotta cheese
2 eggs
1½ cups (120g) coarsely grated
    parmesan cheese
¼ cup finely chopped fresh mint
3 teaspoons finely chopped fresh thyme
2 teaspoons finely chopped fresh rosemary
250g (8 ounces) cannelloni tubes
creamy tomato sauce
1 tablespoon olive oil
1 medium brown onion (150g),
    chopped finely
4 cloves garlic, crushed
1.6kg (3¾ pounds) canned diced tomatoes
½ cup (125ml) pouring cream
1 teaspoon white (granulated) sugar

1 Make creamy tomato sauce.
2 Meanwhile, preheat oven to 180°C/350°F.
3 Cook washed, drained (not dried) spinach in heated large saucepan, stirring, until wilted. Drain; when cool enough to handle, squeeze out excess moisture.
4 Combine spinach in large bowl with ricotta, eggs, ½ cup of the parmesan and the herbs; season. Using a large piping bag, fill cannelloni tubes with spinach mixture.
5 Spread a third of the tomato sauce into shallow 25cm x 35cm (10-inch x 14-inch) ovenproof dish; place tubes in dish, in single layer, then top with remaining sauce.
6 Bake cannelloni, covered, 20 minutes. Uncover, sprinkle with remaining parmesan; bake about 15 minutes or until pasta is tender and cheese is browned lightly.
creamy tomato sauce Heat oil in large saucepan; cook onion, stirring, until softened. Add garlic; cook, stirring, until fragrant. Add undrained tomatoes; bring to the boil. Reduce heat; simmer, uncovered, stirring occasionally, about 20 minutes or until sauce thickens slightly. Cool 10 minutes; blend or process sauce with cream and sugar until smooth. Season to taste.

MUSHROOM RISOTTO

prep + cook time **1 hour** serves **6**

nutritional count per serving **15.7g total fat**
(3.3g saturated fat); 1781kJ (426 cal);
55.2g carbohydrate; 16.8g protein; 3.3g fibre

3 cups (750ml) chicken stock
1 litre (4 cups) water
2 tablespoons olive oil
1 small brown onion (80g), chopped finely
10g (½ ounce) butter
2 cloves garlic, sliced thinly
100g (3 ounces) shiitake mushrooms,
    sliced thinly
100g (3 ounces) button mushrooms,
    sliced thinly
100g (3 ounces) oyster mushrooms,
    sliced thinly
2 cups (400g) arborio rice
½ cup (125ml) dry white wine
75g (2½ ounces) baby spinach leaves
⅓ cup (25g) coarsely grated
    parmesan cheese
⅓ cup (50g) roasted pine nuts
¼ cup finely chopped fresh chives

1 Place stock and the water in large
saucepan; bring to the boil. Reduce heat;
simmer, covered.
2 Heat oil in large saucepan; cook onion,
stirring, until softened. Add butter, garlic and
mushrooms; cook, stirring, until mushrooms
soften. Add rice; stir rice to coat in mushroom
mixture. Add wine; cook, stirring until liquid is
almost evaporated.
3 Stir in 1 cup simmering stock mixture; cook,
stirring, over low heat until liquid is absorbed.
Continue adding stock mixture, in 1-cup
batches, stirring, until absorbed after each
addition. Total cooking time should be about
35 minutes or until rice is tender.
4 Stir spinach and cheese into risotto.
Remove from heat; stir in nuts and half the
chives. Season to taste. Serve sprinkled with
remaining chives.

fettuccine carbonara

FETTUCCINE CARBONARA

prep + cook time **30 minutes** serves **4**

nutritional count per serving **66.7g total fat**
(39g saturated fat); 3662kJ (876 cal);
33.6g carbohydrate; 53.7g protein; 2.4g fibre

500g (1 pound) fresh fettuccine pasta
60g (2 ounces) butter
6 rindless bacon slices (390g), sliced thinly
1 clove garlic, crushed
½ teaspoon cracked black pepper
1¼ cups (310ml) pouring cream
2 eggs, beaten lightly
½ cup (40g) finely grated parmesan cheese
½ cup (40g) finely grated romano cheese
2 teaspoons coarsely chopped fresh chives

1 Cook pasta in large saucepan of boiling
water until tender; drain.
2 Meanwhile, melt butter in medium frying pan;
cook bacon, stirring, about 5 minutes.
3 Add garlic, pepper and cream to pan;
simmer, uncovered, until sauce reduces by half.
Remove from heat. Stir in egg and cheeses.
4 Add pasta to sauce; stir to coat. Serve pasta
sprinkled with chives.

tip It is fine to use just one 300ml carton of cream.

mushroom risotto

LEMON, PEA AND RICOTTA PASTA

prep + cook time **15 minutes** serves **4**
nutritional count per serving **15.6g total fat**
(4.7g saturated fat); 2123kJ (508 cal);
69g carbohydrate; 19g protein; 6.9g fibre

Cook 375g (12 ounces) angel hair pasta in large saucepan of boiling water until tender; add 2 cups frozen peas during last minute of pasta cooking time. Drain, reserving ¼ cup cooking liquid. Meanwhile, heat 2 tablespoons olive oil in small frying pan; cook 2 thinly sliced garlic cloves, stirring, until fragrant. Combine pasta and peas in large bowl with reserved cooking liquid, garlic, 2 teaspoons finely grated lemon rind and ½ cup lemon juice; stir in ¾ cup crumbled ricotta cheese. Season to taste.

tips Fetta cheese can be used in place of the ricotta cheese. And ⅓ cup loosely packed fresh mint leaves makes a nice addition. If you don't have angel hair pasta, you can use thin or regular spaghetti, instead.

FETTUCCINE ALLE VONGOLE

prep + cook time **30 minutes** serves **4**
nutritional count per serving **11.3g total fat**
(1.8g saturated fat); 2023kJ (484 cal);
67.7g carbohydrate; 17.5g protein; 4.1g fibre

Heat 2 tablespoons olive oil in large saucepan; cook 3 crushed garlic cloves and 1 finely chopped fresh long red chilli, stirring, 1 minute. Add 1 tablespoon rinsed and drained baby capers, ¾ cup dry white wine, ¾ cup fish stock and 2 tablespoons lemon juice; bring to the boil. Add 1kg (2 pounds) clams; cook vongole mixture, covered, about 5 minutes or until clams open. Meanwhile, cook 375g (12 ounces) fettuccine pasta in large saucepan of boiling water until tender; drain. Add pasta, ½ cup coarsely chopped fresh flat-leaf parsley and ¼ cup coarsely chopped fresh chives to vongole mixture; toss gently. Season to taste.

PASTA FAVOURITES

SPAGHETTI WITH OIL AND GARLIC

prep + cook time **15 minutes** serves **4**
nutritional count per serving **19.6g total fat**
(2.8g saturated fat); 2454kJ (587 cal);
85.5g carbohydrate; 14.2g protein; 4.6g fibre

Cook 500g (1 pound) spaghetti in large
saucepan of boiling water until tender; drain.
Meanwhile, heat ⅓ cup olive oil in large frying
pan; cook 3 crushed garlic cloves, stirring, until
golden brown. Stir in 2 tablespoons finely
chopped fresh flat-leaf parsley. Combine garlic
mixture with pasta; season to taste.

tip **A good quality olive oil will make this dish even
more delicious.**

RAVIOLI WITH SPINACH AND SAGE

prep + cook time **25 minutes** serves **4**
nutritional count per serving **49g total fat**
(28.8g saturated fat); 2475kJ (592 cal);
21.4g carbohydrate; 16.1g protein; 3.2g fibre

Cook 500g (1 pound) ricotta and spinach
ravioli in large saucepan of boiling water until
tender; drain, return pasta to pan. Meanwhile,
place 1¼ cups pouring cream and ¼ cup finely
grated parmesan cheese in small saucepan;
bring to the boil. Reduce heat; simmer,
uncovered, about 5 minutes or until
mixture thickens slightly. Add cream mixture,
100g (3½ ounces) baby spinach leaves and
1 tablespoon small sage leaves to pasta;
toss gently. Season to taste. Divide pasta
between serving plates; top with 2 tablespoons
roasted pine nuts and 2 tablespoons flaked
parmesan cheese.

tip **It is fine to use just one 300ml carton of cream.**

CHICKEN CACCIATORE WITH GREMOLATA AND PARMESAN TOPPING

prep + cook time 1 hour 50 minutes serves 6
nutritional count per serving 29.1g total fat
(8.6g saturated fat); 2019kJ (483cal);
19g carbohydrate; 31.4g protein; 3.8g fibre

1.5kg (3 pounds) chicken pieces
⅓ cup (50g) plain (all-purpose) flour
2 tablespoons olive oil
1 large red onion (300g), chopped coarsely
2 cloves garlic, crushed
1 medium red capsicum (bell pepper) (200g),
    sliced thickly
½ cup (125ml) dry white wine
410g (13 ounces) canned diced tomatoes
410g (13 ounces) canned cherry tomatoes
    in tomato juice
½ cup (125ml) chicken stock
2 tablespoons tomato paste
1 teaspoon caster (superfine) sugar
½ cup (60g) seeded black olives
gremolata and parmesan topping
½ cup (40g) coarsely grated
    parmesan cheese
⅓ cup finely chopped fresh flat-leaf parsley
1 tablespoon finely grated lemon rind
1 clove garlic, crushed

1 Preheat oven to 200°C/400°F.
2 Coat chicken in flour; shake off excess. Heat oil in large deep flameproof casserole dish; cook chicken, in batches, until browned. Remove from dish.
3 Cook onion, garlic and capsicum in same dish, stirring, until onion softens. Add wine; simmer, uncovered, until liquid is reduced by half. Stir in undrained tomatoes, stock, paste and sugar.
4 Return chicken to dish; bring to the boil. Cover; bake 45 minutes. Uncover; bake about 45 minutes or until chicken is tender and sauce has thickened. Skim fat from surface; stir in olives. Season to taste.
5 Meanwhile, make gremolata and parmesan topping. Sprinkle over dish just before serving.
gremolata and parmesan topping Combine ingredients in small bowl.

MAINS

BARBECUED SEAFOOD

prep + cook time **1 hour (+ refrigeration)** serves **8**
nutritional count per serving **8.7g total fat**
(1.7g saturated fat); 836kJ (200 cal);
1.3g carbohydrate; 28.5g protein; 0.4g fibre

16 uncooked medium king prawns
   (shrimp) (720g)
1 teaspoon finely grated lemon rind
½ teaspoon dried chilli flakes
1 clove garlic, crushed
1 tablespoon finely chopped fresh oregano
2 tablespoons olive oil
8 slices prosciutto (120g)
8 butterflied sardines (240g)
280g (9 ounces) baby octopus, quartered
200g (6½ ounces) squid hoods, sliced
   into rings
2 tablespoons balsamic vinegar
¼ cup coarsely chopped fresh
   flat-leaf parsley
500g (1 pound) small black mussels
¼ cup (60ml) lemon juice
1 medium tomato (150g), seeded,
   chopped finely

1 Remove and discard prawn heads. Cut prawns lengthways, three-quarters of the way through and down to 1cm (½ inch) before the tail, leaving shells intact; press prawns down on board to flatten.
2 Combine prawns, rind, chilli, garlic, oregano and half the oil in medium bowl. Cover; refrigerate 1 hour.
3 Wrap a prosciutto slice firmly around each sardine.
4 Cook octopus and squid on heated oiled grill plate (or grill or barbecue). Combine octopus and squid in medium heatproof bowl with remaining oil, vinegar and 2 tablespoons of the parsley. Cover to keep warm.
5 Cook prawns and sardines on heated oiled grill plate (or grill or barbecue).
6 Meanwhile, cook mussels, covered, on heated oiled flat plate about 5 minutes or until mussels open. Place mussels in medium heatproof bowl; drizzle with juice, sprinkle with tomato and remaining parsley. Serve seafood with lemon wedges, if you like.

tip You can buy butterflied sardines from most good fish markets, or get your fishmonger to butterfly the fish for you. To butterfly your own fish, buy an already gutted fish, slice down the length of the belly until just before the tail, place fish, belly-down, on a chopping board and roll gently with a rolling pin several times to flatten, pull head gently up and away towards the tail, removing head and bones together.

QUAIL WITH RADICCHIO AND PEAR SALAD

prep + cook time **45 minutes** serves **4**
nutritional count per serving **25.1g total fat**
(9g saturated fat); 1522kJ (364 cal);
13.6g carbohydrate; 19.4g protein; 3.9g fibre

4 quails (640g)
16 fresh sage leaves
4 slices prosciutto (60g), halved lengthways
2 teaspoons olive oil
1 ruby red grapefruit (350g)
40g (1½ ounces) butter
2 small pears (360g), cut into wedges
2 small radicchio (300g), leaves separated
balsamic dressing
2 tablespoons balsamic vinegar
1 tablespoon olive oil
1 clove garlic, crushed

1 Using kitchen scissors, cut along sides of each quail's backbone; discard backbones. Halve each quail along breastbone. Place 2 sage leaves on each quail half; wrap with slice of prosciutto.
2 Heat oil in large frying pan; cook quail, in batches, about 10 minutes or until cooked.
3 Meanwhile, segment grapefruit over small bowl; reserve 1 tablespoon of juice for dressing.
4 Make balsamic dressing.
5 Heat butter in medium frying pan; add pear, cook about 4 minutes or until tender.
6 Divide radicchio, grapefruit and pear between serving plates; top with quail, drizzle with dressing.
balsamic dressing Combine vinegar, oil, garlic and reserved grapefruit juice in screw-top jar; season, shake well.

SEAFOOD SALAD WITH SALSA VERDE

prep + cook time **45 minutes** serves **4**
nutritional count per serving **17.9g total fat**
(2.8g saturated fat); 1626kJ (389 cal);
3.6g carbohydrate; 52.2g protein; 2g fibre

500g (1 pound) large uncooked king
  prawns (shrimp)
250g (8 ounces) scallops, roe removed
500g (1 pound) cleaned whole baby
  octopus, halved
500g (1 pound) large black mussels
90g (3 ounces) baby spinach leaves
salsa verde
⅔ cup finely chopped fresh flat-leaf parsley
½ cup each finely chopped fresh mint
  and basil
2 cloves garlic, chopped finely
1 tablespoon drained capers, rinsed,
  chopped finely
3 drained anchovy fillets, chopped finely
¼ cup (60ml) olive oil
1 tablespoon red wine vinegar
1 teaspoon dijon mustard

1 Make salsa verde.
2 Shell and devein prawns leaving tails
intact. Combine prawns, scallops and
octopus in large bowl with half the salsa verde.
3 Scrub mussels, remove beards; cook
mussels on heated oiled barbecue plate
(or grill or grill pan) until mussels open.
Remove from heat.
4 Add prawn mixture to heated oiled barbecue
plate; cook, turning, until mixture is cooked.
5 Serve seafood on spinach; drizzle with
remaining salsa verde.
salsa verde Combine ingredients in medium
bowl; season to taste.

tip **Serve salad with lemon wedges and toasted bread.**

SEARED TUNA WITH KIPFLER SMASH AND SALSA VERDE

prep + cook time **45 minutes** serves **4**
nutritional count per serving **58.2g total fat**
(14g saturated fat); 3570kJ (854 cal);
28.5g carbohydrate; 51.8g protein; 4.5g fibre

1kg (2 pounds) kipfler (fingerling) potatoes,
peeled, halved
30g (1 ounce) butter
1 tablespoon extra virgin olive oil
4 x 175g (5½-ounce) tuna steaks
80g (2½ ounces) baby rocket (arugula) leaves
salsa verde
½ cup firmly packed fresh flat-leaf
parsley leaves
¼ cup loosely packed fresh mint leaves
⅔ cup (160ml) extra virgin olive oil
¼ cup (50g) drained capers, rinsed
2 teaspoons dijon mustard
2 tablespoons lemon juice
8 drained anchovy fillets
1 clove garlic, quartered

1 Boil, steam or microwave potato until
tender; drain. Using potato masher, crush
potato roughly in large bowl with butter and
oil. Cover to keep warm.
2 Meanwhile, make salsa verde.
3 Cook fish, in batches, on heated oiled grill
plate (or grill or barbecue) until browned both
sides and cooked as desired.
4 Divide rocket and potato between serving
plates; top with fish, drizzle with salsa verde.
salsa verde Blend or process ingredients until
just combined. Transfer to medium jug; season
to taste, whisk before pouring over fish.

tips If the kipfler potatoes that you purchase for this
recipe are young and quite small, scrubbing them well
(rather than peeling) will be sufficient. Tuna is at its best
if browned both sides but still fairly rare in the middle;
overcooking will make it dry.

VEAL SCALLOPINE WITH POTATO AND FENNEL GRATIN

prep + cook time **1 hour 35 minutes** serves **4**
nutritional count per serving **48.7g total fat**
(25.2g saturated fat); 3114kJ (745 cal);
22.9g carbohydrate; 51.7g protein; 2.9g fibre

400g (12½ ounces) potatoes
1 small fennel bulb (200g), sliced thinly
3 teaspoons plain (all-purpose) flour
1¼ cups (310ml) pouring cream
2 tablespoons milk
20g (¾ ounce) butter
⅓ cup (25g) coarsely grated
    parmesan cheese
½ cup (35g) stale breadcrumbs
2 tablespoons olive oil
8 veal schnitzels (800g)
2 tablespoons lemon juice
¼ cup (60ml) dry white wine
1 clove garlic, crushed
¾ cup (180ml) chicken stock
1 teaspoon dijon mustard
2 tablespoons drained baby capers, rinsed
¼ cup coarsely chopped fresh
    flat-leaf parsley

1 Preheat oven to 180°C/350°F. Oil deep
1-litre (4-cup) baking dish.
2 Using sharp knife, mandoline or V-slicer, cut
potatoes into very thin slices; pat dry with
absorbent paper. Layer a third of the potato
into prepared dish; top with half the fennel.
Continue layering remaining potato and fennel,
finishing with potato.
3 Blend flour with a little of the cream in
medium jug to form a smooth paste; stir in milk
and remaining cream, season. Pour cream
mixture over potato; dot with butter. Cover with
foil; bake about 45 minutes or until vegetables
are just tender. Uncover dish, sprinkle with
combined cheese and breadcrumbs; bake
about 20 minutes or until top is browned lightly.
4 During last 15 minutes of gratin cooking
time, heat oil in large frying pan; cook veal, in
batches, until cooked as desired. Remove from
pan; cover to keep warm.
5 Add juice, wine and garlic to same pan;
bring to the boil. Reduce heat; simmer,
uncovered, until liquid is reduced by half.
Add stock and mustard; simmer, uncovered,
5 minutes. Remove from heat; stir in capers
and parsley, season to taste. Serve veal topped
with sauce and accompanied by gratin.

tips We used the creamy white, all-purpose sebago
potato in this gratin but you can substitute it with
desiree, spunta or any good baking potato, one that
keeps its shape during cooking. Don't peel or slice the
potatoes until you're ready to assemble the dish, and
make sure you pat the slices dry with absorbent paper.
It's fine to use one 300ml carton of cream for this recipe.

OSSO BUCCO WITH POLENTA CRUST

prep + cook time **2 hours 20 minutes** serves **8**
nutritional count per serving **15.3g total fat**
(6.3g saturated fat); 1705kJ (408 cal);
26.7g carbohydrate; 36.5g protein; 3.4g fibre

8 pieces veal osso bucco (1.4kg)
⅓ cup (50g) plain (all-purpose) flour
2 tablespoons olive oil
30g (1 ounce) butter
1 large brown onion (200g), chopped finely
1 large carrot (180g), chopped finely
1 stalk celery (150g), chopped finely
4 cloves garlic, crushed
½ cup (125ml) dry white wine
800g (1½ pounds) canned crushed tomatoes
2 sprigs fresh rosemary
1 cup (250ml) chicken stock
1 tablespoon finely chopped fresh
    flat-leaf parsley
2 teaspoons finely grated lemon rind
polenta crust
2 cups (500ml) milk
2 cups (500ml) water
1 cup (150g) instant polenta
½ cup (40g) finely grated parmesan cheese
1 egg, beaten lightly

1 Preheat oven to 200°C/400°F.

2 Coat veal in flour; shake off excess. Heat half the oil and half the butter in large flameproof baking dish; cook veal, in batches, until browned. Remove from dish.

3 Heat remaining oil and butter in same dish; cook onion, carrot, celery and garlic, stirring, until onion softens. Add wine; boil, uncovered, until liquid has evaporated. Return veal to dish with undrained tomatoes, rosemary and stock; bring to the boil. Season. Cover tightly with foil; bake 1½ hours.

4 Meanwhile, make polenta crust.

5 Remove dish from oven; discard veal bones and rosemary. Break meat into large chunks. Divide veal mixture among eight oiled 1¼-cup (310ml) ovenproof dishes; top with polenta crust mixture. Place dishes on oven tray; bake, uncovered, about 25 minutes or until browned lightly. Serve sprinkled with combined parsley and rind.

polenta crust Combine milk and the water in medium saucepan; bring almost to the boil. Gradually add polenta, stirring. Reduce heat; cook, stirring, about 5 minutes or until polenta thickens slightly. Remove from heat, stir in cheese and egg; season to taste.

tip **The dishes in this picture are not individual serves – each dish here will serve four.**

fish with fennel and lemon mint vinaigrette

STICKY LEMON AND CHILLI PORK RIBS WITH HERB SALAD

prep + cook time **50 minutes (+ refrigeration)** serves **4**
nutritional count per serving **31g total fat**
(9.2g saturated fat); 2646kJ (633 cal);
7.1g carbohydrate; 79.7g protein; 3g fibre

1.2kg (2½ pounds) pork belly ribs
2 tablespoons olive oil
1 tablespoon finely grated lemon rind
1 tablespoon finely chopped fresh oregano
1 tablespoon caster (superfine) sugar
1 teaspoon dried chilli flakes
white bean puree
400g (12½ ounces) canned white beans,
    rinsed, drained
2 tablespoons each lemon juice and
    hot water
1 clove garlic, crushed
herb salad
1 cup loosely packed fresh flat-leaf
    parsley leaves
½ cup loosely packed fresh small
    basil leaves
⅓ cup loosely packed fresh oregano leaves
125g (4 ounces) grape tomatoes, halved
1 tablespoon lemon juice
2 teaspoons olive oil

1 Combine ribs with remaining ingredients in large bowl; season. Cover; refrigerate 3 hours or overnight.
2 Cook ribs on heated oiled barbecue (or grill or grill pan) about 20 minutes. Remove ribs from barbecue; cover, stand 5 minutes.
3 Make white bean puree; make herb salad.
4 Serve ribs with puree and salad.
white bean puree Blend or process ingredients until smooth; season to taste.
herb salad Combine ingredients in medium bowl; season to taste.

FISH WITH FENNEL AND LEMON MINT VINAIGRETTE

prep + cook time **25 minutes** serves **4**
nutritional count per serving **8.8g total fat**
(2g saturated fat); 1074kJ (257 cal);
3.2g carbohydrate; 39.3g protein; 2.7g fibre

2 medium fennel bulbs (600g)
1 tablespoon olive oil
2 tablespoons lemon juice
⅓ cup firmly packed fresh mint leaves,
    chopped finely
1 tablespoon white wine vinegar
4 white fish steaks (750g)

1 Discard stalk from fennel; cut bulb into quarters and remove core.
2 Combine oil, juice, mint and vinegar in small bowl. Brush fennel with some of the oil mixture. Cook fennel on heated oiled barbecue (or grill or grill pan) about 10 minutes, turning often.
3 Meanwhile, brush fish with some of the oil mixture; cook on heated oiled barbecue, brushing with more oil mixture during cooking.
4 Serve fish and fennel drizzled with remaining oil mixture and roasted cherry truss tomatoes, if you like.

sticky lemon and chilli pork ribs with herb salad

braised pork with fresh sage

BRAISED PORK WITH FRESH SAGE

prep + cook time **1 hour 45 minutes** serves **6**
nutritional count per serving **18.6g total fat**
(10.3g saturated fat); 1488kJ (356 cal);
3.7g carbohydrate; 31.8g protein; 2g fibre

90g (3 ounces) butter
1.5kg (3-pound) rack of pork (6 cutlets),
   rind removed
2 medium carrots (240g), sliced thickly
6 baby onions (150g), peeled
4 cloves garlic, peeled
2 dried bay leaves
6 sprigs fresh thyme
1⅓ cups (330ml) dry white wine
⅓ cup (80ml) dry white wine, extra
⅓ cup (80ml) chicken stock
1 tablespoon fresh small sage leaves

1 Preheat oven to 180°C/350°F.
2 Heat butter in large flameproof dish; cook pork until browned all over. Remove from dish.
3 Add carrot, onions, garlic, bay leaves and thyme to dish; cook, stirring, about 5 minutes or until browned lightly. Return pork to dish with wine; season. Transfer to oven; cook about 1¼ hours or until cooked as desired. Remove pork; cover to keep warm.
4 Strain cooking liquid into small saucepan; discard vegetables. Add extra wine and stock to pan; bring to the boil. Reduce heat; simmer, uncovered, 5 minutes. Stir in sage.
5 Serve pork with sage sauce, and roasted baby new potatoes and cherry truss tomatoes, if you like.

tip **Ask your butcher to remove the rind and tie the pork well. Roast the salted rind on a rack in a hot oven until crisp. Serve with the pork.**

veal marsala

VEAL MARSALA

prep + cook time **25 minutes** serves **4**
nutritional count per serving **12.3g total fat**
(6.9g saturated fat); 1471kJ (351 cal);
5.6g carbohydrate; 45.5g protein; 0.2g fibre

45g (1½ ounces) butter
8 veal schnitzels (800g)
2 shallots (50g), chopped finely
2 teaspoons plain (all-purpose) flour
½ cup (125ml) marsala
½ cup (125ml) beef stock

1 Heat half the butter in large frying pan; cook veal, in batches, until cooked as desired. Remove from pan; cover to keep warm.
2 Heat remaining butter in same pan; cook shallot, stirring, until softened. Add flour; cook, stirring, 2 minutes. Stir in marsala; bring to the boil. Reduce heat; simmer, uncovered, 2 minutes. Add stock; bring to the boil. Reduce heat; simmer, uncovered, about 4 minutes or until sauce is reduced by half.
3 Serve veal topped with sauce; serve with zucchini, if you like.

gorgonzola and sage-stuffed chicken

EGGPLANT PARMIGIANA

prep + cook time **1 hour 15 minutes** serves **6**
nutritional count per serving **13.2g total fat**
(5.5g saturated fat); 1041kJ (249 cal);
16.9g carbohydrate; 13.4g protein; 5.6g fibre

2 medium eggplants (600g)
2 teaspoons coarse cooking salt
  (kosher salt)
1 tablespoon olive oil
1 medium brown onion (150g),
  chopped finely
2 cloves garlic, crushed
2 tablespoons finely chopped fresh basil
2⅔ cups (700g) bottled tomato pasta sauce
1½ cups (150g) coarsely grated
  mozzarella cheese
½ cup (40g) finely grated parmesan cheese
½ cup (35g) stale breadcrumbs

1 Peel and discard strips of skin from
eggplant; cut eggplant into 5mm (¼-inch)
slices. Place eggplant in colander; sprinkle with
salt. Stand in sink 30 minutes. Rinse eggplant
under cold water; drain. Squeeze excess water
from eggplant.
2 Meanwhile, heat oil in medium saucepan;
cook onion, garlic and basil, stirring, until onion
softens. Add sauce; bring to the boil. Reduce
heat; simmer, uncovered, about 15 minutes or
until sauce thickens slightly. Season to taste.
3 Preheat oven to 220°C/425°F. Oil six
1¼-cup (310ml) ovenproof dishes.
4 Spoon half the sauce into dishes; top with
half the eggplant and half the mozzarella. Top
with remaining eggplant, remaining sauce, then
remaining mozzarella. Sprinkle with combined
parmesan and breadcrumbs.
5 Cover dishes with foil; place on oven tray.
Bake about 40 minutes or until eggplant is
tender. Uncover; bake about 15 minutes or
until browned lightly.

tip The dishes in this picture are not individual serves
– each dish here will serve three.

GORGONZOLA
AND SAGE-STUFFED CHICKEN

prep + cook time **35 minutes** serves **4**
nutritional count per serving **24.3g total fat**
(10.3g saturated fat); 1940kJ (464 cal);
4.8g carbohydrate; 55.5g protein; 2.1g fibre

⅓ cup (50g) semi-dried tomatoes in oil
4 chicken breast fillets (800g)
125g (4 ounces) gorgonzola cheese,
  cut into four slices
12 fresh sage leaves
8 slices pancetta (120g)
75g (2½ ounces) baby rocket (arugula) leaves

1 Drain tomatoes; reserve 2 tablespoons
of the oil.
2 Cut horizontal slits into chicken fillets,
three-quarters of the way through, to
make pockets.
3 Divide cheese, sage and tomatoes between
pockets in chicken; wrap two slices of pancetta
around each chicken fillet.
4 Cook chicken in heated oiled large frying pan
until cooked through.
5 Toss rocket with reserved oil, season to
taste; serve with thickly sliced chicken.

eggplant parmigiana

char-grilled lamb cutlets with white bean puree and tapenade

CHAR-GRILLED LAMB CUTLETS WITH WHITE BEAN PUREE AND TAPENADE

prep + cook time **45 minutes** serves **4**
nutritional count per serving **25.6g total fat**
(9g saturated fat); 1438kJ (344 cal);
8g carbohydrate; 21.1g protein; 5g fibre

800g (1½ pounds) canned white beans,
    rinsed, drained
1 cup (250ml) chicken stock
1 clove garlic, crushed
1 tablespoon pouring cream
2 tablespoons lemon juice
2 tablespoons olive oil
¼ cup (60g) black olive tapenade
12 french-trimmed lamb cutlets (600g)
300g (9½ ounces) baby spinach leaves

1 Combine beans and stock in medium saucepan; bring to the boil. Reduce heat; simmer, uncovered, about 15 minutes or until liquid is absorbed. Transfer to medium bowl; mash beans with garlic, cream, juice and one tablespoon of the oil until smooth. Season to taste. Cover to keep warm.
2 Meanwhile, combine tapenade with remaining oil in small bowl.
3 Cook cutlets, in batches, on heated oiled grill plate (or grill or barbecue) until browned both sides and cooked as desired; cover to keep warm.
4 Boil, steam or microwave spinach until wilted; drain.
5 Divide bean puree, spinach and cutlets among serving plates; drizzle with tapenade mixture.

tip Many varieties of white beans are available canned, among them cannellini, butter and haricot beans. Any of these are suitable for this puree. Drain beans then rinse well under cold water before using them. We find that cooking them briefly with a little liquid results in a more luscious, creamier puree.

italian-style lamb cutlets

ITALIAN-STYLE LAMB CUTLETS

prep + cook time **30 minutes** serves **4**
nutritional count per serving **11.1g total fat**
(5.8g saturated fat); 790kJ (189 cal);
3.1g carbohydrate; 18.8g protein; 1.2g fibre

8 french-trimmed lamb cutlets (400g)
125g (4 ounces) firm goat's
    cheese, crumbled
¼ cup (35g) finely chopped drained
    sun-dried tomatoes
2 tablespoons finely shredded fresh basil
4 slices prosciutto (60g), halved lengthways

1 Cut a small horizontal slit in the side of each lamb cutlet.
2 Combine cheese, tomatoes and basil in medium bowl; season. Press cheese mixture into lamb pockets. Wrap each cutlet with a slice of prosciutto.
3 Cook cutlets in heated oiled large frying pan until browned both sides and cooked through.

LEMON-PEPPER LAMB WITH MINTED BROAD BEAN RISONI

prep + cook time **55 minutes (+ refrigeration)** serves **4**
nutritional count per serving **17.2g total fat**
(4.6g saturated fat); 2190kJ (524 cal);
37.4g carbohydrate; 53.6g protein; 10.4g fibre

1 tablespoon finely grated lemon rind
1 tablespoon cracked black pepper
2 teaspoons sea salt
1 clove garlic, sliced thinly
2 tablespoons olive oil
4 lamb backstraps (eye of loin) (800g)
500g (1 pound) frozen broad (fava) beans
¾ cup (165g) risoni pasta
4 green onions (scallions), sliced thinly
⅔ cup coarsely chopped fresh
    flat-leaf parsley
½ cup coarsely chopped fresh mint
2 tablespoons lemon juice

1 Combine rind, pepper, salt, garlic and half the oil in large bowl, add lamb; turn lamb to coat in lemon-pepper mixture. Cover; refrigerate 1 hour.
2 Meanwhile, place beans in large heatproof bowl, cover with boiling water; stand 10 minutes. Drain beans; when cool enough to handle, peel away grey skins.
3 Cook pasta in large saucepan of boiling water until tender; drain. Rinse under cold water; drain.
4 Meanwhile, heat remaining oil in large frying pan; cook lamb until cooked as desired. Remove from pan, cover; stand 5 minutes then slice thickly.
5 Cook onion in same pan, stirring, until softened. Add pasta and beans; cook, stirring, until heated through. Remove from heat; stir in herbs and juice. Season to taste. Serve broad bean risoni with lamb.

tip A small rice-sized pasta, risoni is most often used in hearty soups, as is its near relative, the slightly larger orzo, which means "barley" in Italian. Both small pastas are also often used as a substitute for rice and other grains in casseroles and bakes.

creamy polenta with slow-roasted mushrooms

CREAMY POLENTA WITH SLOW-ROASTED MUSHROOMS

prep + cook time **1 hour** serves **4**
nutritional count per serving **17.8g total fat**
(8.5g saturated fat); 1622kJ (388 cal);
39g carbohydrate; 18.6g protein; 9.1g fibre

155g (5 ounces) oyster mushrooms, halved
200g (6½ ounces) fresh shiitake
    mushrooms, halved
200g (6½ ounces) swiss brown
    mushrooms, halved
2 large flat mushrooms (160g),
    chopped coarsely
280g (9 ounces) vine-ripened tomatoes,
    chopped coarsely
1 small red onion (100g), sliced thinly
2 cloves garlic, sliced thinly
1 tablespoon olive oil
15g (½ ounce) dried porcini mushrooms
1 cup (250ml) boiling water
2 cups (500ml) milk
1 cup (250ml) cold water
¾ cup (125g) polenta
20g (¾ ounce) butter
⅓ cup (35g) finely grated parmesan cheese
1 cup firmly packed fresh flat-leaf
    parsley leaves
½ cup coarsely chopped fresh chives

1 Preheat oven to 160°C/325°F.
2 Combine oyster, shiitake, swiss brown
and flat mushrooms in large baking dish
with tomato, onion, garlic and oil; season.
Roast about 30 minutes or until mushrooms
are tender.
3 Meanwhile, soak porcini in the boiling water
in small jug for 15 minutes. Drain over small
bowl; reserve liquid. Chop porcini finely.
4 Bring reserved porcini liquid, milk and the
cold water to the boil in medium saucepan.
Gradually add polenta, stirring. Reduce heat;
cook, stirring, about 5 minutes or until polenta
thickens slightly. Stir in porcini, butter and
cheese; season to taste.
5 Stir herbs into mushroom mixture. Divide
polenta between serving plates; top with
mushroom mixture.

tomato, olive and ricotta tart

TOMATO, OLIVE AND RICOTTA TART

prep + cook time **30 minutes** serves **4**
nutritional count per serving **25.1g total fat**
(12.5g saturated fat); 1965kJ (470 cal);
46.9g carbohydrate; 11.5g protein; 5.8g fibre

2 sheets puff pastry
¾ cup (110g) coarsely chopped
    semi-dried tomatoes
¾ cup (90g) seeded black olives
½ cup (120g) ricotta cheese, crumbled
½ small red onion (50g), sliced thinly
¼ cup loosely packed fresh basil leaves, torn
1 egg, beaten lightly

1 Preheat oven to 200°C/400°F. Line oven tray
with baking paper.
2 Cut a 16cm x 24cm (6½-inch x 9½-inch)
rectangle from pastry; place on oven tray.
Top with tomatoes, olives, cheese, onion and
basil, leaving a 2cm (¾-inch) border on all
sides; brush a little of the egg around edges.
3 Cut an 18cm x 24cm (7-inch x 9½-inch)
rectangle from remaining pastry sheet; score
pastry in a diamond pattern. Place scored
pastry over filling, press edges to seal; brush
pastry with egg.
4 Bake tart 20 minutes or until golden brown.

beef fillet with gremolata
and semi-dried tomato polenta

1 Lightly oil 22cm (9-inch) square cake pan.
2 Combine the water and stock in large saucepan; bring to the boil. Gradually add polenta, stirring. Reduce heat; cook, stirring constantly, about 10 minutes or until polenta thickens. Stir in tomato and cheese; season to taste. Spread polenta into prepared pan. Cover; refrigerate about 1 hour or until firm.
3 Meanwhile, make gremolata.
4 Cook beef in heated oiled large frying pan until browned all over and cooked as desired. Remove from pan, cover; stand 10 minutes then slice thickly.
5 Meanwhile, turn polenta onto board; cut into four squares, cut each square diagonally into two triangles. Cook polenta triangles in same pan, in batches, until browned lightly both sides.
6 Divide polenta between serving plates; top with beef then gremolata.
gremolata Combine ingredients in small bowl.

BEEF FILLET WITH GREMOLATA AND SEMI-DRIED TOMATO POLENTA

prep + cook time **40 minutes (+ refrigeration)** serves 4
nutritional count per serving **10.2g total fat**
(4g saturated fat); 1154kJ (276 cal);
29.8g carbohydrate; 33.8g protein; 4.1g fibre

1½ cups (375ml) water
1½ cups (375ml) vegetable stock
¾ cup (120g) polenta
⅓ cup (75g) semi-dried tomatoes, chopped coarsely
2 tablespoons finely grated parmesan cheese
500g (1-pound) piece beef eye fillet
gremolata
½ cup coarsely chopped fresh flat-leaf parsley
¼ cup (60ml) lemon juice
1 tablespoon finely grated lemon rind
1 clove garlic, crushed

VEAL SALTIMBOCCA

prep + cook time **35 minutes** serves 4
nutritional count per serving **24g total fat**
(13.1g saturated fat); 2312kJ (553 cal);
9g carbohydrate; 63.3g protein; 3.6g fibre

8 veal schnitzels (800g)
8 slices prosciutto (120g)
4 bocconcini cheeses (240g), sliced thinly
⅔ cup (100g) drained semi-dried tomatoes
16 fresh sage leaves
40g (1½ ounces) butter
1 cup (250ml) dry white wine
1 tablespoon lemon juice
2 tablespoons coarsely chopped fresh sage

1 Top each piece of veal with prosciutto, cheese, tomatoes and sage leaves. Fold in half to secure filling; secure with toothpicks or small skewers.
2 Heat half the butter in medium frying pan; cook veal, in batches, until cooked as desired. Remove from pan; cover to keep warm.
3 Add wine to same pan; bring to the boil. Boil, uncovered, until wine reduces by half. Stir in remaining butter, juice and sage.
4 Serve saltimbocca drizzled with sauce.

veal saltimbocca

TIRAMISU

prep time 25 minutes (+ refrigeration) **serves** 6
nutritional count per serving 70.4g total fat
(45.5g saturated fat); 3536kJ (846 cal);
42.9g carbohydrate; 6.7g protein; 1.4g fibre

2 tablespoons ground espresso coffee
1 cup (250ml) boiling water
½ cup (125ml) marsala
250g (8 ounces) packet sponge
    finger (lady finger) biscuits
1¼ cups (310ml) thickened (heavy) cream
¼ cup (40g) icing (confectioners') sugar
2 cups (500g) mascarpone cheese
2 tablespoons marsala, extra
50g (1½ ounces) dark eating (semi-sweet)
    chocolate, grated coarsely

1 Combine coffee and the boiling water in
coffee plunger; stand 2 minutes before
plunging. Combine coffee mixture and marsala
in medium heatproof bowl; cool 10 minutes.
2 Place a third of the biscuits, in single layer,
over base of deep 2-litre (8-cup) dish; drizzle
with a third of the coffee mixture.
3 Beat cream and sifted icing sugar in small
bowl with electric mixer until soft peaks form;
transfer to large bowl. Fold in combined cheese
and extra marsala.
4 Spread a third of the cream mixture over
biscuits in dish. Submerge half the remaining
biscuits, one at a time, in coffee mixture; place
over cream layer. Top biscuit layer with half the
remaining cream mixture. Repeat process with
remaining biscuits, coffee mixture and cream
mixture; sprinkle with chocolate. Cover;
refrigerate 3 hours or overnight.

tips Savoiardi, from the Piedmont region of Italy, are
the traditional sponge-cake-like biscuits used in making
a tiramisu. They're also used in making other semifreddi
and charlottes. Be certain the ones you buy are crisp; if
soft, they've passed their use-by date. It is fine to use
just one 300ml carton of cream for this recipe.

CHOCOLATE HAZELNUT GELATO

prep + cook time **40 minutes (+ cooling & freezing)**
serves **8**
nutritional count per serving **58.6g total fat**
(27g saturated fat); 2909kJ (696 cal);
32.8g carbohydrate; 10g protein; 2.2g fibre

1 cup (140g) hazelnuts
1⅔ cups (410ml) milk
2⅓ cups (580ml) pouring cream
6 egg yolks
⅓ cup (75g) caster (superfine) sugar
¾ cup (250g) chocolate hazelnut spread

1 Preheat oven to 180°C/350°F.
2 Place nuts in small shallow baking dish; roast, uncovered, about 8 minutes or until skins begin to split. Place nuts in clean tea towel; rub vigorously to remove skins. Discard skins; chop nuts coarsely.
3 Bring milk, cream and nuts to the boil in medium saucepan; remove from heat, cover.
4 Whisk egg yolks and sugar in medium bowl until creamy; gradually whisk hot milk mixture into egg mixture. Return mixture to same pan; stir over low heat, without boiling, until custard mixture thickens slightly. Add chocolate spread; whisk until combined.
5 Strain custard into large heatproof bowl; discard nuts. Cover surface of custard with plastic wrap; cool then refrigerate about 1 hour or until cold.
6 Pour custard into a shallow container, such as an aluminium slab cake pan, cover with foil, freeze until almost firm. Place mixture in large bowl, chop coarsely then beat with electric mixer until smooth. Pour into deep container, cover; freeze until firm. Repeat process two more times (or pour custard into ice-cream maker, churn according to manufacturer's instructions). Freeze until firm.
7 Serve gelato in ice-cream cones, if you like.

white chocolate panna cotta with passionfruit sauce

WHITE CHOCOLATE PANNA COTTA WITH PASSIONFRUIT SAUCE

prep + cook time **30 minutes (+ refrigeration)** serves **6**
nutritional count per serving **28.7g total fat
(18.6g saturated fat); 1751kJ (419 cal);
35.6g carbohydrate; 5.5g protein; 2.9g fibre**

**1¼ cups (310ml) thickened (heavy) cream
¾ cup (180ml) milk
150g (4½ ounces) white eating chocolate,
    chopped coarsely
⅓ cup (75g) caster (superfine) sugar
2 teaspoons gelatine
1 tablespoon water
½ cup (125ml) passionfruit pulp
1 cup (250ml) sauternes-style dessert wine**

1 Grease six ½-cup (125ml) non-metallic
moulds.
2 Stir cream, milk, chocolate and 2 tablespoons
of the sugar in small saucepan over heat,
without boiling, until smooth.
3 Sprinkle gelatine over the water in small
heatproof jug. Stand jug in small saucepan of
simmering water; stir until gelatine dissolves.
Stir into cream mixture.
4 Divide mixture between moulds; cover,
refrigerate about 3 hours or until set.
5 Meanwhile, bring passionfruit, wine and
remaining sugar to the boil in small saucepan.
Reduce heat; simmer, uncovered, without
stirring, about 10 minutes or until passionfruit
syrup reduces by a third. Cool.
6 Turn panna cotta onto serving plates; drizzle
with passionfruit syrup.

tips **It is fine to use just one 300ml carton of cream for
this recipe. Sauternes is a dessert wine from the region
of the same name in western France – serve the
remaining dessert wine with the panna cotta. You will
need about six passionfruit for this recipe. Panna cotta
can be made a day ahead; store, covered, in refrigerator.
Wipe the outsides of panna cotta moulds with a hot cloth
to make turning them out onto serving plates easier.**

grapefruit and campari granita

GRAPEFRUIT AND CAMPARI GRANITA

prep + cook time **20 minutes (+ cooling & freezing)**
serves **6**
nutritional count per serving **0.3g total fat
(0g saturated fat); 594kJ (142 cal);
39.3g carbohydrate; 0.9g protein; 0.1g fibre**

**½ cup (110g) caster (superfine) sugar
1 cup (250ml) water
2 tablespoons finely grated ruby red or pink
    grapefruit rind
1 litre (4 cups) ruby red or pink grapefruit
    juice, strained
½ cup (125ml) campari**

1 Stir sugar and the water in medium
saucepan over heat, without boiling, until sugar
dissolves. Bring to the boil; boil, uncovered,
about 3 minutes or until thickened slightly; cool.
2 Stir rind, juice and campari into sugar
mixture. Pour mixture into a shallow pan, cover
with foil; freeze until firm. Stir occasionally with
a fork during freezing.
3 Using fork, shave granita into individual
glasses to serve.

BLOOD ORANGE SORBET

prep + cook time **30 minutes (+ freezing)** serves **8**
nutritional count per serving **0g total fat**
(0g saturated fat); 497kJ (119 cal);
30.2g carbohydrate; 0.6g protein; 0.1g fibre

Stir 2 tablespoons finely grated blood orange
rind, 1 cup caster (superfine) sugar and
2½ cups water in medium saucepan over heat,
without boiling, until sugar dissolves; bring to
the boil. Reduce heat; simmer, uncovered,
without stirring, 5 minutes. Transfer to large
heatproof jug, cool to room temperature; stir in
1 cup blood orange juice. Pour sorbet mixture
into loaf pan, cover with foil; freeze 3 hours or
overnight. Process mixture with 1 egg white
until smooth. Return to loaf pan, cover; freeze
until firm. Serve sprinkled with extra orange
rind, if desired.

CHOCOLATE ZABAGLIONE

prep + cook time **15 minutes** serves **4**
nutritional count per serving **5.8g total fat**
(2g saturated fat); 385kJ (92 cal);
19.9g carbohydrate; 3.4g protein; 0.1g fibre

Combine 4 egg yolks and ⅓ cup caster
(superfine) sugar in medium heatproof bowl.
Place bowl over medium saucepan of
simmering water, ensuring that the water
doesn't touch bottom of bowl. Beat with
electric mixer until thick and creamy. Gradually
beat in combined ⅓ cup marsala and
3 teaspoons sifted cocoa powder, beating
constantly, further 5 minutes or until mixture
is thick and creamy. Spoon mixture into four
⅔-cup (160ml) serving glasses.

tip **Zabaglione should be made just before serving.**

DESSERT FAVOURITES

AFFOGATO WITH FRANGELICO

prep time **10 minutes** serves **6**
nutritional count per serving **13.5g total fat**
(8.6g saturated fat); 1045kJ (250 cal);
23.2g carbohydrate; 3.9g protein; 0g fibre

Place ⅓ cup ground espresso coffee
beans and 1½ cups boiling water in coffee
plunger; stand 4 minutes before plunging.
Place 2 scoops vanilla ice-cream in each of
six small heatproof glasses or coffee cups;
pour 1 tablespoon frangelico over each.
Pour over hot coffee; serve immediately.

tip While we used a hazelnut-flavoured liqueur in this
recipe, you could use your favourite liqueur – orange
and/or chocolate flavours also work well with coffee.

MIXED BERRY BRUSCHETTA

prep + cook time **15 minutes** serves **6**
nutritional count per serving **47.6g total fat**
(29.8g saturated fat); 2725kJ (652 cal);
46.4g carbohydrate; 9.9g protein; 3.3g fibre

Beat 1¼ cups thickened (heavy) cream and
1 tablespoon sifted icing (confectioner's) sugar
in small bowl with electric mixer until soft peaks
form; fold in 250g (8 ounces) mascarpone
cheese. Preheat grill (broiler). Place 6 thick
slices brioche under grill until lightly toasted
both sides. Serve brioche topped with
mascarpone mixture and 150g (5 ounces)
each raspberries and blueberries. Sprinkle with
shredded fresh mint, if you like.

tip It is fine to use just one 300ml carton of cream for
this recipe.

ARTICHOKES

globe large flower-bud; a member of the thistle family; it has tough petal-like leaves, and is edible in part when cooked.

hearts tender centre of the globe artichoke; is obtained after the choke is removed. Cooked hearts are available in brine or marinated in oil.

BACON SLICES also called bacon rashers.

BAKING POWDER a raising agent consisting of two parts cream of tartar to one part bicarbonate of soda (baking soda).

BAY LEAVES aromatic leaves from the bay tree available fresh or dried; adds a strong, slightly peppery flavour.

BEANS

broad also called fava, windsor and horse beans; available dried, fresh, canned and frozen. Fresh should be peeled twice (discard outer green pod and beige-green inner shell); the frozen beans have had their pods removed but the beige shell still needs removal.

white a generic term we use for canned or dried cannellini, haricot, navy or great northern beans.

BEEF EYE-FILLET also known as beef tenderloin; fine textured, extremely tender and expensive.

BICARBONATE OF SODA also called baking soda.

BLOOD ORANGE a citrus fruit with blood-red streaked rind and flesh; sweet, non-acidic, salmon-coloured pulp and juice with slight strawberry or raspberry overtones. The rind is not as bitter as an ordinary orange.

BREADCRUMBS

packaged fine-textured but crunchy white breadcrumbs; good for coating foods that are to be fried.

stale crumbs made by grating, blending or processing one- or two-day-old bread.

BRIOCHE French in origin; a rich, yeast-leavened, cake-like bread made with butter and eggs. Available from cake or specialty bread shops.

BUTTER we use salted butter unless stated.

CAPERS grey-green buds of a warm climate shrub, sold dried and salted or pickled in a vinegar brine; tiny young ones (baby capers) are available in brine or dried in salt.

CAPSICUM also called pepper or bell pepper.

CHEESE

bocconcini from the diminutive of "boccone", meaning 'mouthful' in Italian; walnut-sized, baby mozzarella, a delicate, semi-soft, white cheese. Sold fresh, it spoils rapidly; refrigerate in brine for one or two days.

fetta Greek in origin; a crumbly textured goat's- or sheep's-milk cheese with a sharp, salty taste.

goat's made from goat's milk; has an earthy, strong taste. Available soft, crumbly and firm, in various shapes and sizes, and sometimes rolled in ash or herbs.

gorgonzola a creamy Italian blue cheese with a mild, sweet taste; good as an accompaniment to fruit or used to flavour sauces.

mascarpone an Italian fresh cultured-cream product made similarly to yogurt. White to creamy yellow in colour, with a buttery-rich, luscious texture. Is soft, creamy and spreadable.

mozzarella soft, spun-curd cheese; traditionally made from water-buffalo

milk. Now generally made from cow's milk, it is the most popular pizza cheese because of its low melting point and elasticity when heated.

parmesan also called parmigiano; a hard, grainy cow's-milk cheese originating in the Parma region of Italy. The curd is salted in brine for a month then aged for up to 2 years.

pizza cheese a commercial blend of grated mozzarella, cheddar and parmesan.

ricotta soft, sweet, moist, white cow's-milk cheese with a low fat content (8.5 per cent) and a slightly grainy texture. Its name roughly translates as "cooked again" and refers to ricotta's manufacture from a whey that is itself a by-product of other cheese making.

CHICKEN

breast fillet breast halved, skinned, boned.

small chicken also called spatchcock or poussin; no more than six weeks old, weighing a maximum of 500g. Spatchcock is also a cooking term to describe splitting poultry open, flattening and grilling.

CHICKPEAS also called garbanzos, hummus or channa; an irregularly round, sandy-coloured legume. Available canned or dried (needs several hours soaking in cold water before use).

CHILLI use rubber gloves when handling fresh chillies as they can burn your skin. We use unseeded chillies as the seeds contain the heat.

flakes also sold as crushed chilli; dehydrated deep-red extremely fine slices and whole seeds.

CHOCOLATE

dark eating also called semi-sweet or luxury chocolate; contains a high percentage of cocoa liquor and cocoa butter, and little added sugar. Unless stated otherwise, we use dark eating chocolate in this book as it's ideal for use in desserts and cakes.

white eating contains no cocoa solids but derives its sweet flavour from cocoa butter. Very sensitive to heat.

CHOCOLATE HAZELNUT

SPREAD also known as Nutella; made of cocoa powder, hazelnuts, sugar and milk.

CIABATTA meaning 'slipper' in Italian, the traditional shape of this popular crisp-crusted, open-textured white sourdough bread.

CLOVES dried flower buds of a tropical tree; used whole or ground. They have a strong scent and taste so use sparingly.

COCOA POWDER also known as unsweetened cocoa.

CORNFLOUR also called cornstarch. Made from corn or wheat.

CREAM we use fresh pouring cream, also known as pure cream. It has no additives, and contains a minimum fat content of 35 per cent.

thickened a whipping cream that contains a thickener (minimum fat content of 35 per cent).

CUMIN also called zeera or comino; resembling caraway in size, cumin is the dried seed of a parsley-related plant with a spicy, almost curry-like flavour. Available dried as seeds or ground.

DILL also called dill weed; used fresh or dried, in seed form or ground. Its feathery, frond-like fresh leaves are grassier and more subtle than the dried version or the seeds.

EGGPLANT also called aubergine. Ranging in size from tiny to very large and in colour from pale green to deep purple. Can also be purchased char-grilled, packed in oil, in jars.

EGGS we use large (60g) chicken eggs unless stated otherwise. If a recipe calls for raw or barely cooked eggs, exercise caution if there is a salmonella problem in your area, particularly in food eaten by children and pregnant women.

FENNEL also called finocchio or anise; a crunchy green vegetable slightly resembling celery. Dried fennel seeds are also available; they have a stronger licorice flavour.

FIGS are best eaten in peak season, at the height of summer. They vary in skin and flesh colour according to type not ripeness. When ripe, figs should be unblemished.

FLOUR

plain unbleached wheat flour is the best for baking: the gluten content ensures a strong dough, which produces a light result.

self-raising also called self-rising; plain or wholemeal flour with baking powder and salt added; make at home in the proportion of 1 cup flour to 2 teaspoons baking powder.

GELATINE we use dried (powdered) gelatine; it's also available in sheet form called leaf gelatine. Three teaspoons of dried gelatine (8g or one sachet) is about the same as four sheets.

HAZELNUTS also called filberts; grape-sized, rich, sweet nut with a brown skin. Remove skin by rubbing heated nuts together vigorously in a tea towel.

LENTILS dried pulses often identified by and named after their colour (red, brown, yellow).

MARSALA a fortified Italian wine produced in the region surrounding the Sicilian city of Marsala; recognisable by its intense amber colour and complex aroma. Often used in cooking.

MILK we use full-cream homogenised milk unless stated otherwise.

MUSHROOMS

button small, cultivated white mushrooms with a mild flavour. When a recipe in this book calls for an unspecified mushroom, use button.

flat large and flat with a rich earthy flavour.

oyster also called abalone; grey-white and shaped like a fan. Prized for its smooth texture and subtle, oyster-like flavour. Also available pink.

porcini, dried also called cèpes; the richest-flavoured mushrooms. Expensive, but because they're so strongly flavoured, only a small amount is required.

shiitake, fresh also called chinese black, forest or golden oak mushrooms. Although cultivated, they have the earthiness and taste of wild mushrooms. They are large and meaty.

swiss brown also called roman or cremini. Light to dark brown mushrooms with full-bodied flavour.

OREGANO also called wild marjoram; has a woody stalk and clumps of tiny, dark-green leaves. Has a pungent, peppery flavour.

PAPRIKA ground dried, sweet red capsicum (bell pepper); varieties available include sweet, hot, mild and smoked.

PASTA

angel hair also known as *capelli d'angelo* ('angel hair' in Italian); thin, extremely delicate strands of pasta, usually paired with a light sauce or simple flavours.

cannelloni large tubes of pasta, available fresh or dried, usually filled with a meat, cheese or vegetable mixture and then baked.

fettuccine fresh or dried ribbon pasta made from durum wheat, semolina and egg. Also available plain or flavoured.

penne Italian for 'pen', named after their shape, resembling a quill, and has angled ends and ridges; also available in a smooth variety.

ravioli squares of pasta stuffed with cheese, vegetables or meat. Usually made from fresh pasta either by hand or in moulds.

risoni small rice-shape pasta; very similar to another small pasta, orzo.

spaghetti long, thin solid strands of pasta.

POLENTA also known as cornmeal; a flour-like cereal made of dried corn (maize).

PROSCIUTTO unsmoked Italian ham; salted, air-cured and aged, it is usually eaten uncooked.

QUAIL related to the pheasant and partridge; a small, delicate-flavoured farmed game bird ranging in weight from 250g to 300g.

RICE, ARBORIO small, round grain rice well-suited to absorb a large amount of liquid; the high level of starch makes it suitable for risottos, giving the dish its classic creaminess.

SEAFOOD

mussels should only be bought from a reliable fish market: they must be tightly closed when bought, indicating they are alive. Before cooking, scrub shells with a strong brush to remove beards.

octopus usually tenderised before you buy them; both octopus and squid require either long slow cooking (for large molluscs) or quick cooking over high heat (for small molluscs) – anything in between will make the octopus tough and rubbery.

squid also called calamari; a type of mollusc. Buy squid hoods to make preparation and cooking faster.

SHALLOTS also called french shallots, golden shallots or eschalots. Small and elongated, with a brown skin, they grow in tight clusters similar to garlic.

SPONGE FINGER BISCUITS also called savoiardi, savoy biscuits or lady's fingers, they are Italian-style crisp fingers made from sponge cake mixture.

SUGAR

caster also called superfine or finely granulated table sugar.

icing also known as confectioners' sugar or powdered sugar; pulverised granulated sugar crushed together with a small amount of cornflour.

light brown also known simply as brown, a soft, finely granulated sugar retaining molasses for colour and flavour.

pure icing also called confectioners' sugar or powdered sugar.

TOMATO

bottled pasta sauce a prepared sauce; often a blend of tomatoes, herbs and spices.

cherry also called tiny tim or tom thumb; small and round.

paste triple-concentrated tomato puree used to flavour soups, stews, sauces and casseroles.

puree canned pureed tomatoes (not tomato paste); substitute with fresh peeled and pureed tomatoes.

semi-dried partially dried tomato pieces in olive oil; softer and juicier than sun-dried, these are not preserved so do not keep as long as sun-dried.

sun-dried tomato pieces dried with salt; this dehydrates the tomato, concentrating the flavour. We use sun-dried tomatoes in oil, unless stated otherwise.

VANILLA

bean dried, long, thin pod; the minuscule black seeds inside are used to impart a vanilla flavour.

extract obtained from vanilla beans infused in water; a non-alcoholic version of essence.

VEAL, OSSO BUCCO also called veal shin, usually cut into 3cm to 5cm thick slices and used in the famous Italian slow-cooked casserole of the same name.

VINEGAR

balsamic originally from Modena, Italy, there are now many on the market ranging in pungency and quality depending on how, and for how long, they have been aged. Quality can be determined up to a point by price; use the most expensive sparingly.

YEAST (dried and fresh), a raising agent. Granular (7g sachets) and fresh (20g blocks) yeast can almost always be used interchangeably.

ZUCCHINI also called courgette; harvested when young, its edible flowers can be stuffed and deep-fried.

CONVERSION CHART

MEASURES

One Australian metric measuring cup holds approximately 250ml, one Australian metric tablespoon holds 20ml, one Australian metric teaspoon holds 5ml.

The difference between one country's measuring cups and another's is within a 2- or 3-teaspoon variance, and will not affect your cooking results. North America, New Zealand and the United Kingdom use a 15ml tablespoon. All cup and spoon measurements are level. The most accurate way of measuring dry ingredients is to weigh them. When measuring liquids, use a clear glass or plastic jug with metric markings.

We use large eggs with an average weight of 60g.

DRY MEASURES

METRIC	IMPERIAL
15g	½oz
30g	1oz
60g	2oz
90g	3oz
125g	4oz (¼lb)
155g	5oz
185g	6oz
220g	7oz
250g	8oz (½lb)
280g	9oz
315g	10oz
345g	11oz
375g	12oz (¾lb)
410g	13oz
440g	14oz
470g	15oz
500g	16oz (1lb)
750g	24oz (1½lb)
1kg	32oz (2lb)

LIQUID MEASURES

METRIC	IMPERIAL
30ml	1 fluid oz
60ml	2 fluid oz
100ml	3 fluid oz
125ml	4 fluid oz
150ml	5 fluid oz
190ml	6 fluid oz
250ml	8 fluid oz
300ml	10 fluid oz
500ml	16 fluid oz
600ml	20 fluid oz
1000ml (1 litre)	1¾ pints

LENGTH MEASURES

METRIC	IMPERIAL
3mm	⅛in
6mm	¼in
1cm	½in
2cm	¾in
2.5cm	1in
5cm	2in
6cm	2½in
8cm	3in
10cm	4in
13cm	5in
15cm	6in
18cm	7in
20cm	8in
23cm	9in
25cm	10in
28cm	11in
30cm	12in (1ft)

OVEN TEMPERATURES

These oven temperatures are only a guide for conventional ovens.
For fan-forced ovens, check the manufacturer's manual.

	°C (CELSIUS)	°F (FAHRENHEIT)
Very slow	120	250
Slow	150	275-300
Moderately slow	160	325
Moderate	180	350-375
Moderately hot	200	400
Hot	220	425-450
Very hot	240	475

The imperial measurements used in these recipes are approximate only. Measurements for cake pans are approximate only.

A

affogato with frangelico 73
angel hair pasta with smoked
  salmon and asparagus 31
antipasto
  arancini 4
  artichokes with lemon caper
    dressing 6
  cherry tomato & parmesan dip 10
  chunky olive and herb dip 10
  giardiniera (pickled vegetables) 9
  marinated mushrooms 6
  melon in prosciutto 11
  warm olives with chilli 11
arancini 4
artichokes with lemon caper
  dressing 6
asparagus, baked, risotto 26

B

balsamic dressing 43
beans
  bean salad with mozzarella,
    sun-dried tomato and olives 18
  white bean puree 52
beef
  carpaccio 14
  fillet with gremolata and
    semi-dried tomato polenta 64
berry, mixed, bruschetta 73
blood orange sorbet 72
bruschetta
  mixed berry 73
  tomato, basil and capers, with 14

C

caprese salad with figs 20
carbonara, fettuccine 34
char-grilled lamb cutlets with white
  bean puree and tapenade 59
chicken
  cacciatore with gremolata and
    parmesan topping 38
  gorgonzola and sage-stuffed 56
chocolate
  chocolate hazelnut gelato 68
  white chocolate panna cotta with
    passionfruit sauce 71
  zabaglione 72

creamy polenta with slow-roasted
  mushrooms 63
creamy tomato sauce 32

D

desserts
  affogato with frangelico 73
  blood orange sorbet 72
  chocolate hazelnut gelato 68
  chocolate zabaglione 72
  grapefruit and campari
    granita 71
  mixed berry bruschetta 73
  tiramisu 66
  white chocolate panna cotta with
    passionfruit sauce 71
dips
  cherry tomato & parmesan 10
  chunky olive and herb dip 10
dressing
  balsamic 43
  italian 18

E

eggplant parmigiana 56

F

fennel and ricotta pizza 25
fettuccine alle vongole 36
fettuccine carbonara 34
fig
  caprese salad with 20
  fig & prosciutto salad 21
  fig, prosciutto and goat's cheese
    pizzettas 22
fish with fennel and lemon mint
  vinaigrette 52

G

giardiniera (pickled vegetables) 9
gelato, chocolate hazelnut 68
gorgonzola and sage-stuffed
  chicken 56
grapefruit and campari granita 71
gremolata 64
gremolata and parmesan
  topping 38

H

herb salad 52

I

italian dressing 18
italian-style lamb cutlets 59

L

lamb
  char-grilled cutlets with white
    bean puree and tapenade 59
  cutlets, italian-style 59
  lemon-pepper lamb with minted
    broad bean risoni 60
lemon, pea and ricotta pasta 36
lemon-pepper lamb with minted
  broad bean risoni 60

M

mains
  barbecued seafood 40
  braised pork with fresh sage 55
  chicken cacciatore with gremolata
    and parmesan topping 38
  creamy polenta with slow roasted
    mushrooms 62
  eggplant parmigiana 56
  fish with fennel and lemon mint
    vinaigrette 52
  gorgonzola and sage-stuffed
    chicken 56
  italian-style lamb cutlets 59
  lamb cutlets, char-grilled with
    white bean puree and
    tapenade 59
  lemon-pepper lamb with minted
    broad bean risoni 60
  olive and ricotta tart 63
  osso bucco with polenta crust 51
  quail with radicchio and pear
    salad 43
  seafood salad with salsa verde 44
  sticky lemon and chilli pork ribs
    with herb salad 52
  tomato, olive and ricotta tart 63
  tuna, seared, with kipfler smash
    and salsa verde 47

INDEX

veal marsala 55
veal saltimbocca 64
veal scallopine with potato and
    fennel gratin 48
melon in prosciutto 11
mushrooms
    creamy polenta with slow roasted
      mushrooms 62
    marinated 6
    mushroom & pancetta salad 20
    risotto 34

O
olives
    chunky olive and herb dip 10
    tomato, olive and ricotta tart 63
    warm olives with chilli 11
osso bucco with polenta crust 51

P
panna cotta, white chocolate, with
    passionfruit sauce 71
pasta
    angel hair, with smoked salmon
      and asparagus 31
    fettuccine alle vongole 36
    fettuccine carbonara 34
    lemon, pea and ricotta 36
    ravioli with spinach and sage 37
    ricotta gnocchi with tomato
      sauce 28
    spaghetti napoletana 28
    spaghetti with oil and garlic 37
    spinach and ricotta cannelloni 32
pizzas
    dough 22, 25
    fennel and ricotta 25
    fig, prosciutto and goat's cheese
      pizzettas 22
    potato and rosemary 25
polenta
    beef fillet with gremolata and
      semi-dried tomato polenta 64
    creamy, with slow roasted
      mushrooms 62
    crust 51

pork
    braised, with fresh sage 55
    sticky lemon and chilli pork ribs
      with herb salad 52
potato and rosemary pizza 25
prawn and asparagus risotto 31

Q
quail with radicchio and pear salad 43

R
ravioli with spinach and sage 37
ricotta
    lemon, pea and ricotta pasta 36
    ricotta gnocchi with tomato
      sauce 28
    tomato, olive and ricotta tart 63
risotto
    baked asparagus 26
    mushroom 34
    prawn and asparagus 31
rocket & parmesan salad 21

S
salads
    bean salad with mozzarella,
      sun-dried tomato and olives 18
    caprese salad with figs 20
    fig & prosciutto 21
    herb 52
    mushroom & pancetta 20
    rocket & parmesan 21
    seafood with salsa verde 44
salsa verde 44
sauce, creamy tomato 32
sardine skewers with
    gremolata dressing 17
seafood
    angel hair pasta with smoked
      salmon and asparagus 31
    barbecued 40
    fettuccine alle vongole 36
    fish with fennel and lemon mint
      vinaigrette 52
    prawn and asparagus risotto 31
    sardine skewers with gremolata
      dressing 17

    seafood salad with salsa verde 44
    tuna, seared, with kipfler smash
      and salsa verde 47
sicilian zucchini flowers 12
sorbet, blood orange 72
spaghetti
    napoletana 28
    with oil and garlic 37
spinach and ricotta cannelloni 32
starters
    beef carpaccio 14
    bruschetta with tomato, basil
      and capers 14
    sardine skewers with gremolata
      dressing 17
    sicilian zucchini flowers 12
sticky lemon and chilli pork ribs
    with herb salad 52

T
tiramisu 66
tomato
    bruschetta with tomato basil and
      capers 14
    caprese salad with figs 20
    cherry tomato & parmesan dip 10
    creamy tomato sauce 32
    tomato, olive and ricotta tart 63
    tuna, seared, with kipfler smash
      and salsa verde 47

V
veal
    marsala 55
    saltimbocca 64
    scallopine with potato and
      fennel gratin 48

W
white bean puree 52
white chocolate panna cotta with
    passionfruit sauce 71

Z
zabaglione, chocolate 72
zucchini flowers, sicilian 12

First Published in 2011 by ACP Magazines Ltd,

a division of Nine Entertainment Co.

54 Park St, Sydney

GPO Box 4088, Sydney, NSW 2001.

phone (02) 9282 8618; fax (02) 9267 9438

acpbooks@acpmagazines.com.au; www.acpbooks.com.au

ACP BOOKS

General Manager · Christine Whiston

Associate Publisher · Seymour Cohen

Editor-in-Chief · Susan Tomnay

Creative Director · Hieu Chi Nguyen

Food Director · Pamela Clark

Published and Distributed in the United Kingdom by Octopus Publishing Group

Endeavour House

189 Shaftesbury Avenue

London WC2H 8JY

United Kingdom

phone (+44)(0)207 632 5400; fax (+44)(0)207 632 5405

info@octopus-publishing.co.uk;

www.octopusbooks.co.uk

Printed by Toppan Printing Co., China

International foreign language rights, Brian Cearnes, ACP Books bcearnes@acpmagazines.com.au

A catalogue record for this book is available from the British Library.

ISBN 978-1-907428-44-9

© ACP Magazines Ltd 2011

ABN 18 053 273 546